LOOK ON THE BRIGHT SIDE

Sophie Golding

LOOK ON THE BRIGHT SIDE

Text by Lucy York

Design by Luci Ward

An Hachette UK Company
www.hachette.co.uk

Vie Books, an imprint of Summersdale Publishers Ltd
Part of Octopus Publishing Group Limited
Carmelite House
50 Victoria Embankment
LONDON
EC4Y 0DZ
UK

www.summersdale.com

Printed and bound in China

ISBN: 978-1-78783-012-7

Substantial discounts on bulk quantities of Summersdale books are available to corporations, professional associations and other organizations. For details contact general enquiries: telephone: +44 (0) 1243 771107 or email: enquiries@summersdale.com.

Success is not final, failure is not fatal:
it is the courage to continue that counts.

AUTHOR UNKNOWN

All through my life I have been tested.
My will has been tested, my courage
has been tested, my strength has been tested.
Now my patience and endurance are
being tested... I have learned to live my life
one step, one breath, and one moment
at a time, but it was a long road.
I set out on a journey of love,
seeking truth, peace, and understanding.
I am still learning.

MUHAMMAD ALI (1942-2016)

If you learn from defeat, you haven't really lost.

ZIG ZIGLAR (1926-2012)

CONTENTS

INTRODUCTION

If someone were to find a way to bottle happiness and sell it to the world, they would be sure to make millions. But while no such instant fix has been discovered, the good news is that it doesn't matter, because you have all the tools you need to live a happy life right inside of you. This book is filled with practical tips and inspirational quotes to help you look on the bright side of life, whatever it may throw at you. Happiness may seem an elusive thing, but there are some simple techniques and behaviours you can engage in to up your cheerfulness levels, and there are methods for positive thinking that can help you to find the good in any given situation. It can be as simple as taking a step back and being more mindful of all the aspects of your life;

whether at home or at work or in your personal
relationships, balance is key. And, of course,
happiness is a gift best shared with others.
While managing our thoughts and time
is important, a happy mind is one that
is well nourished, rested and energized,
so healthy eating, exercise and sleep
have all been covered here, too.
Sometimes it's the little things that make all
the difference, so you'll find some tricks to
bring an instant feeling of joy to your day. And
if all else fails, there are some tried and tested
happiness therapies to have some fun with.
You've chosen to read this book, so you're
already walking on the sunny side of the
path. Now read on and choose to be happy.

HAPPINESS
SKILLS

PRIORITIZE DOING WHATEVER BRINGS YOU JOY

Our day-to-day lives are made up of all the different behaviours and activities that we partake in. All of these affect happiness; some increase it, some decrease it. The more time you spend doing the things that increase your sense of well-being and life purpose, the happier you will be.

Happiness is not something ready-made. It comes from your own actions.

Anonymous

Happy IS AS Happy DOES.

ADOPT A GROWTH MINDSET

If you don't believe that it's possible to increase
your happiness, then you may not even try.
Believe that you can grow and change yourself,
and you will believe that you can be happy.

FIND YOUR PURPOSE IN LIFE

What impact do you see yourself making in the world? Spend some time thinking about what brings meaning to your life. It could be by helping others, either in your day-to-day life or through your work, or by contributing to a wider cause, such as volunteering in beach clean-ups to help raise awareness about plastic pollution.

SPEND SMART

The way you choose to spend your money directly impacts the way you live. Buying a fancy, top-of-the-range car will not bring you lasting happiness. Sure, it might feel good at first, but it won't be long before a new, better model of that car is released and yours doesn't seem quite so swanky anymore. Instead, if you buy a reliable car that simply gets you from A to B, you could use the money you saved to spend on positive experiences. For example, you could visit one of the places on your bucket list, spend time with family by treating them to a day out, or buy a gift for a loved one. By doing so you will make happy memories that will last.

HAPPINESS DEPENDS UPON OURSELVES.

Aristotle

SPEAK UP FOR YOURSELF

If you let people walk all over you, it can lead to unhappiness as your own desires fade into the background. Learn how to assert your own needs and express yourself – you will soon feel happier and more in control of your life. Instead of giving in to the urge to please others, learn to say "no"; don't beat around the bush or offer excuses, as that will just give the other person an opening to persuade you otherwise. Simply say "no" in an assertive but courteous manner.

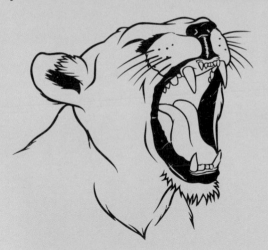

when life
gives you
lemons,

make
lemonade.

REMEMBER THAT
NOTHING LASTS FOREVER

Sometimes we want to escape, to shut out
negative emotions. But sadness and happiness
are two sides of one coin; you can't have one
without the other. Accept sadness when it
comes, but know that it won't last forever.
Embrace happiness all the more when
it arrives for that very same reason.

PAY ATTENTION
TO THE GOOD

Everything we experience can be bad
if we choose to see it that way. By
actively seeking out the benefits of
any situation, you may be surprised
to discover a lot of good. The more
you practise this, the more you will
increase the positive and decrease
the negative in your life.

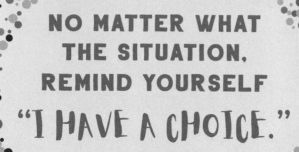

NO MATTER WHAT THE SITUATION, REMIND YOURSELF "I HAVE A CHOICE."

Deepak Chopra

SAVOUR THE MOMENT

By doing this you can increase your level
of happiness in the present moment, as
well as creating longer-lasting positive
emotions. Focus on the smells, sounds
and sights that you are experiencing,
the interactions with anyone else in the
moment with you. Make a mental note of the
positive emotions that you feel. Afterward,
take some time to reflect on how you
made that moment happen for yourself.

EXPLORE WHAT
HAPPINESS MEANS TO YOU

Everyone defines happiness in different ways. Take
some time out to explore what happiness means, feels
and looks like to you. You could do this by journaling:
note down memories, activities, interactions and
relationships that bring you a sense of contentment
or joy. Or you could create a mood board, collecting
together photographs of places, people and things
that bring you happiness. Once you know what you're
looking for, you'll have an easier time finding it.

RELIVE YOUR HAPPY MEMORIES

Think about a moment in your life that brought you great joy and picture the scene in detail. Try to remember sounds, colours, smells, conversations – anything that makes it vivid and real to you. This will trick the brain into believing it is really happening, triggering the happy emotions associated with that memory.

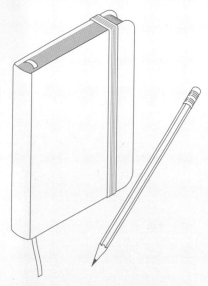

GROW YOUR GRATITUDE

Write down at least five things you are
grateful for in your life. This could include
anything from personal relationships
– maybe there is a dear friend who has
been with you through thick and thin – to
simple things, such as having access to
clean water every day. Seeing these things
down on paper will help to reinforce the
reasons you already have to be happy.

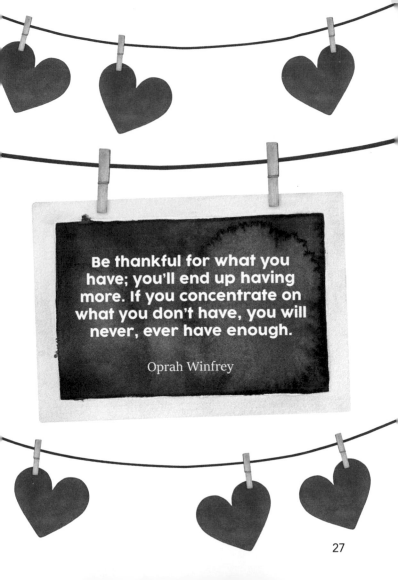

Be thankful for what you have; you'll end up having more. If you concentrate on what you don't have, you will never, ever have enough.

Oprah Winfrey

TRY DOING
THE OPPOSITE

If you want to bring more happiness
into your life, how will you make
that change by doing the same
things you've always done?

For example, if your usual response when someone does something to anger you is to yell at them, try doing a kind deed for them instead. Or if whenever you find yourself in an uncomfortable social situation you flee, try to stick it out. By taking this contrary approach you will disrupt the well-worn pathways in your brain. Just try it and see how it feels.

FINDING HAPPINESS MIGHT INVOLVE TAKING RISKS, BUT THE PRIZE IS WORTH THE GAMBLE.

THINK
POSITIVE

31

START EACH DAY WITH POSITIVE INTENTIONS

Make some time in your morning routine to sit quietly and think about the mindset you want to take with you into the day. This could be a simple word that embodies a positive quality such as "joyfulness", "sharing" or "calm" – or it could be an action: "Smile at strangers" – or an approach: "Today I will not take myself too seriously, I will approach things with a sense of humour."

I think happy, therefore I am happy.

It's been my experience that
you can nearly always enjoy
things if you make up your
mind firmly that you will.

Lucy Maud Montgomery

LET GO OF THE BAD AND WELCOME THE GOOD

If you take stock of your life, you might realize that there are certain bad things that you are holding on to – whether that's memories of bad experiences, negative feelings such as guilt and regret, or bad relationships that are a drain on your energy. Look for ways to let go of these things and make space to welcome new and good experiences, feelings and relationships.

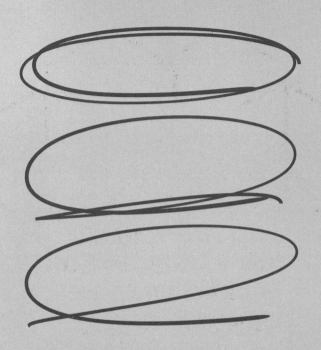

REMEMBER THE GOOD THINGS ABOUT YOURSELF

Write down a list of positive attributes such as kind, honest, creative, dependable, thoughtful, tolerant. Write as many as you can think of. Now look at the list and circle any of the attributes that apply to you.

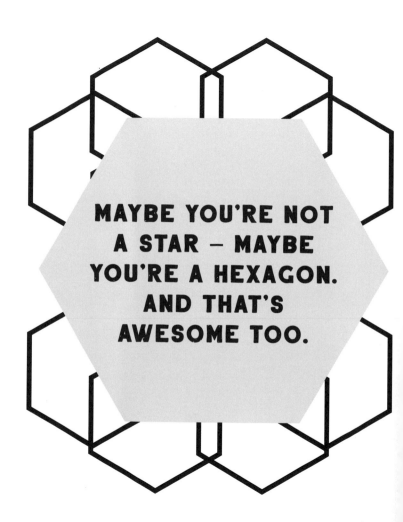

MAYBE YOU'RE NOT A STAR — MAYBE YOU'RE A HEXAGON. AND THAT'S AWESOME TOO.

CELEBRATE THE THINGS
YOU ARE GOOD AT

Maybe you are good at running, listening to others or keeping things organized. By reminding yourself of your strengths, you can make better use of your skills. Make a "Strengths Resumé", listing your key life skills, areas of expertise and accomplishments. Keep adding to it whenever you learn something new or receive a compliment about one of your personal qualities.

STAND UP TO YOUR INNER CRITIC

Have you noticed a negative voice inside your head? The one telling you that you're not good enough, you'll never succeed or that you're unattractive. That's your inner critic, and the first step to removing its power is to note when it comes into play. Are there certain times and situations when it chimes in with negative thoughts? Make a note of these. Once you are aware of your inner critic and how it operates, you will be able to stand up to it.

The second step is to see the inner critic as distinct from yourself. You weren't born with an inner critic. It is a voice that came from outside influences that you have internalized. Once you realize this, you can begin to free yourself from its influence. One technique is to give your inner critic a name. Try giving it a silly name to reduce its potency, like The Old Toad. The third step is to answer back. Whenever your inner critic pipes up, tell it you don't want to hear what it has to say. You'll already feel better by giving yourself a choice in the matter.

POSITIVE ANYTHING

IS BETTER THAN

NEGATIVE NOTHING.

Elbert Hubbard

CULTIVATE
SELF-COMPASSION

We all make mistakes and
sometimes we don't meet our
goals. When things don't turn out
as you hoped, instead of berating
yourself, acknowledge the fact
that you tried – and be satisfied.

STOP SEEKING PERFECTION

Perfection is an impossible goal. Continually
striving toward it will rob you of the satisfaction
of feeling good about everything you have
achieved and are achieving right now. Take
pride in all you do and know that it is enough.

HAPPINESS IS A JOURNEY, NOT A DESTINATION.

NURTURE A POSITIVE SELF-VIEW

When you view yourself negatively, your actions may be unconsciously affected by that internal negativity, which may prevent you from having the happy experiences that you desire. If you feel like you are not worthy of a good relationship, a good job or financial stability, you stop engaging in behaviours that would help you to attain those things. Your negative self-image limits the amount of happiness you can experience. One way you can begin to build a positive self-view is by imagining your best self. Imagination is a powerful thing. When we imagine things, our brains experience them as if they are real. So when you picture yourself as happy, your brain can begin to build pathways that reinforce this view of yourself.

Happiness looks good on you.

STOP COMPARING
YOURSELF TO OTHERS

There will always be someone faster, stronger, better at something or better-looking than you. But there is not one other person in the universe who has your unique blend of skills, qualities and experience – so focus on these personal positives, looking within instead of being distracted by what is going on around you.

FORGET
ABOUT
THE REST.
YOU
DO
YOU.

TAKE A BREAK FROM SOCIAL MEDIA

Social media sites are filled with endless idealistic images, which can affect our self-image. It's easy to feel that everyone is living a better life than yours, but remember that it's not the full picture: people tend to post only the good. No one is living the perfect life; we are all just doing the best we can. Taking a break can help you to refocus on yourself and the positivity in your own life.

VIEW THE
WORLD
WITH AN
OPEN MIND

AND YOU
WILL BE
PLEASANTLY
SURPRISED.

REPLACE NEGATIVITY
WITH POSSIBILITY

When tackling a challenge or trying something
new for the first time, reach for the facts instead
of speculating negatively. Instead of thinking
"I'm useless at running", think "I want to run
a 5K. I know of a training app I can try."

MANAGE YOUR EXPECTATIONS

Tension and disappointment can arise when a situation or experience doesn't turn out the way you expected, especially when you have hyped it up in your imagination by over-planning or over-thinking. Try to foster an attitude of gentle curiosity instead. For example, when planning a trip abroad, think to yourself, "I've always been curious to visit [x destination]. I'm going to go along and see what it's really like there."

The constant
happiness is curiosity.

Alice Munro

SPREAD THE

JOY

THOUSANDS OF CANDLES CAN BE LIT FROM A SINGLE CANDLE,
AND THE LIFE OF THE CANDLE WILL NOT BE SHORTENED.
HAPPINESS NEVER DECREASES BY BEING SHARED.

Buddhist teaching

DO A GOOD DEED

It's a proven fact: doing things for others makes you feel good. So why not boost your own mood and spread a little joy to others in the process? It can be a spontaneous one-off gesture of kindness – offer to walk your neighbour's dog, buy a hot drink for a homeless person on a cold day, help a friend to move house – or you can make it part of your weekly routine by volunteering your time with a charitable organization.

MAKE CONNECTIONS

Did you ever notice that you enjoy things more when you do them with people you love? One of the most important steps you can take toward happiness is building meaningful relationships and social connections. Invest in spending time with family and friends on a weekly basis, creating happy memories together. For example, you could organize a weekly outing with your parents to try out local restaurants. Or if you love hiking, you could arrange a monthly meet-up with friends, tackling a different trail each time.

Smile
at a stranger.

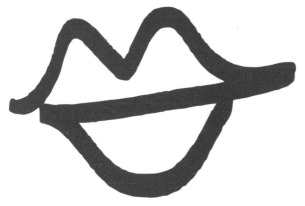

You might just
make their day.

SHARE THE WEALTH

It's true that money can't buy happiness, but by being generous with your funds you can spread a little joy in the world. Buying a gift for a loved one is a simple way to make them feel special and cherished, and knowing that you've done this will make you feel good, too. Or you could make a donation to your favourite charity and have the satisfaction of knowing you've contributed to a good cause.

THERE ARE TWO WAYS OF SPREADING LIGHT: TO BE THE CANDLE, OR THE MIRROR THAT REFLECTS IT.

Edith Wharton

MAKE IT HAPPEN

Don't wait to be invited to social events: be the instigator and organize occasions that bring your friends together. It could be a home movie night, a fun day out or even a trip abroad. You will create happy shared memories that will bring you closer together and that you can reminisce about for years to come.

HUG IT OUT

Fact: giving someone a hug triggers the flow
of oxytocin, a hormone that soothes the
nervous system and lowers blood pressure
and stress levels. So go ahead – reach out
and pull a friend or loved one into a warm
embrace. You'll both feel better right away.

Happy people make other people happy.

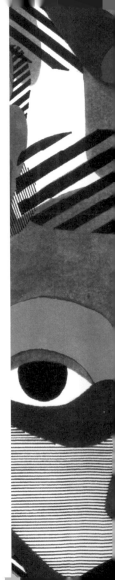

BE A FRIENDLY FACE IN UNFAMILIAR SURROUNDINGS

The next time you find yourself in a new situation where you don't know anyone – perhaps when travelling solo abroad, or at a workshop or social mixer event – instead of waiting for others to befriend you, be the one to make the first move and start a conversation. It's as easy as greeting them with a big smile, introducing yourself and asking a simple question, such as where they come from. They are probably feeling just as nervous as you and will be pleased that someone has taken an interest in getting to know them. You'll benefit twice over – you'll feel more confident and you will have made a new friend.

THE BEST WAY TO CHEER YOURSELF IS TO TRY TO CHEER SOMEBODY ELSE UP.

Mark Twain

RECONNECT WITH A LOVED ONE

Is there someone in your life that you share happy memories with but perhaps don't see that often anymore? Maybe a fun aunt who always came along on your childhood holidays, or a close friend from university who moved abroad? Get in touch to reminisce about the good times and ask how they're doing. Instead of just sending them a quick text, take the time to write a letter or make a phone call. It's guaranteed to make them feel pretty special, which in turn will give you the warm and fuzzies, too.

TELL SOMEONE HOW AWESOME THEY ARE

Paying someone a compliment is guaranteed to boost their mood, and you can feel good about having brought some happy vibes to their day. You might even get a compliment in return.

Let your
happiness
light up the lives
of others.

Let us be grateful
to the people who
make us happy;

they are the
charming gardeners
who make our
souls blossom.

Marcel Proust

SAY "I LOVE YOU"

Say it to your partner, say it to your
family, say it to your friends, and most
importantly, say it to yourself. When
you give love you will receive it
back, and that's something
truly worth feeling
happy about.

HOME IS WHERE
YOU'RE HAPPIEST

MAKE YOUR HOME A SPACE FOR YOUR OWN BRAND OF JOY

Think about how you would like to feel when you are at home. Maybe for you this means decluttering your home and making it a tidy, organized space, within which each item serves a purpose and/or brings you joy; a space where you never have to feel stressed getting ready for work in the morning or preparing meals because everything can easily be found in its rightful place. Or maybe for you it means having a space where you can relax the rules, kick off your shoes after a long day and flop into a comfy old armchair, surrounded by photos of loved ones and happy memories, all the books you've ever read and enjoyed and all the trinkets you've brought back from your adventures abroad. Maybe it's a mixture of the two. The only thing that matters is that your home is a place where you can feel at ease and be yourself.

79

DEDICATE A SPACE TO WHAT YOU ENJOY

If you love to read, you could create a cosy reading nook to curl up in with a good book. If movies are your thing, you could install a home cinema with surround sound. If you're an artistic soul, convert a corner of a room into a creative space with all the tools and materials you need and decorate it with pictures to inspire you.

CREATE A SELF-CARE HAVEN

Think about the things you like to do to take care of yourself and create an environment that encourages those acts of self-care to happen. If you like to take a long relaxing hot bath after a busy day, make your bathroom look as inviting as possible by keeping it squeaky clean and creating a display of scented candles and bath salts to tempt you into running a bath. If taking a nap on the weekend is your way of telling yourself that you've worked hard this week and deserve some extra downtime, you could invest in some cosy blankets and dot them around the lounge and bedroom, so that they're near to hand as a reminder of the permission to snooze when the urge takes you. Or maybe you love to nourish your body with healthy vitamins – you could set up a fruit bowl with a colourful display of fruit in a central location to remind you to reach for one of your five-a-day.

Time you enjoy wasting is not wasted time.

Marthe Troly-Curtin

Take care of
yourself.
You're
worth it.

USE GOOD SCENTS TO
EVOKE GOOD FEELINGS

Studies have shown that certain smells can have
positive psychological effects. Citrus is a well-known
energizing mood booster, vanilla can elevate your
feeling of joy, while lavender can bring calm. Use an
oil burner or scented candles to introduce these scents
into your home. You could also try cooking a favourite
childhood meal to call to mind happy family memories.

The foolish man
seeks happiness
in the distance;
the wise grows it
under his feet.

James Oppenheim

Home is
where
your
heart
feels at
peace.

GET A HOUSE PLANT

The colour green reminds us of nature and is thought to have a calming effect, and leafy plants absorb pollutants from the air. Succulents are a great fun addition to any room and are easy to maintain, while areca palms, rubber plants and philodendrons are proven to be efficient at removing airborne toxins.

UNPLUG, DETOX AND RELAX

The negative effects of too much screen time on your brain and body are well documented. Do your brain a favour by giving it a break from the constant onslaught of information and images brought to it courtesy of social media. Switch off your phone and put it in another room for a few hours while you do something you enjoy or spend time with loved ones. Take a break from watching the TV one evening and read a book or do some home cooking instead.

IF YOU WANT TO BE HAPPY, BE.

Leo Tolstoy

LET THERE BE LIGHT

Researchers have discovered that natural lighting helps people be more productive, happier, healthier and calmer. It has also been proven that natural light can help to regulate seasonal affective disorder (SAD), a type of depression that people experience during specific seasons, typically during the winter when there is less sunlight each day. Throw open those curtains and blinds to let some happy beams of sunlight into your home. Consider carefully the positioning of larger items of furniture so as not to cast shadows or restrict light. Opt for lighter colours on walls to amplify natural light and give a sense of space. A mirror on the wall can make a room feel larger and help reflect light back around the room.

A HAPPY
HOME IS
FILLED
WITH
LOVE.

94

GIVE WARM WELCOMES
AND FOND FAREWELLS

Make a habit of always going to the door to greet
family members, fellow housemates or visitors with
a friendly hug when they arrive in your home, and do
likewise when they leave. As well as helping others to
feel welcome and valued, it will reinforce your own
view of your home as a happy place that's full of love.

WORK HAPPY

CHOOSE A JOB YOU LOVE, AND YOU WILL NEVER HAVE TO WORK A DAY IN YOUR LIFE.

Anonymous

FIND YOUR
WORK–LIFE BALANCE

Sure, work is important, but so is spending
time with friends and loved ones, doing
the activities you enjoy, eating healthily
and exercising. Work is just one part of
the picture of a fulfilling life. Get out your
calendar and schedule in time for all these
areas. Build in slots for prepping healthy
meals, exercising, spending time in the
outdoors and doing activities that you enjoy.

Making these activities automated will
help to form habits that stick. Instigate
a regular slot to spend time with your
loved ones – maybe a Sunday lunch with
family and a weekly friends' night when
you commit to getting together. By making
these arrangements with others you will
provide each other with accountability.

SUNDAY

BUILD GOOD RELATIONSHIPS WITH YOUR COLLEAGUES

It's really worth investing the time and effort on this one. Get to know your fellow teammates – invite them out for lunch or for post-work drinks. Find out what they enjoy and what strengths they bring to the table. You're in this together, after all.

Together we can achieve anything.

BE PLAYFUL

Whatever job you do, even if you love it, there are bound to be some aspects that you enjoy less than others. The trick to getting through those bits is to inject them with a bit of fun. For example, if you are doing repetitive data entry, come up with a scoring system: "Once I've entered ten forms I can stop and make a cup of tea" or "If I get two forms in a row with the name Sarah I get a treat". Or for a practical job, give the equipment you use names and personalities – the sillier the better.

SAY "THANK YOU"

Spread some happy vibes around the workplace by thanking your colleagues for their help. They will feel valued and their resulting smiles will give you a happy boost in turn. Nothing is too small to deserve a thank you – whether it's because they have made you a cup of tea, turned in a piece of work on time or made a positive suggestion in a meeting.

DOING WHAT YOU LIKE IS

FREEDOM.

LIKING WHAT YOU DO IS

HAPPINESS.

Frank Tyger

DO WHAT YOU CAN, BUT NOT TOO MUCH

You're awesome at your job and you can do anything you put your mind to, but don't overload yourself unnecessarily with work in a bid to prove this. Take on only what you are satisfied you can complete to a high standard.

Happiness is the satisfaction of a job well done.

PLEASURE IN
THE JOB PUTS
PERFECTION IN
THE WORK.

Aristotle

TAKE A BREAK

It's easy to get so wrapped up in what you're doing
that you forget to pause, but having some downtime
in the working day is important so that your brain
can recharge. You are more likely to enjoy what
you're doing if you are coming to it from a place
of calm and energy, rather than feeling burned
out. So take a moment. Breathe. Stretch. Relax.

MAKE YOUR WORK
SPACE A HAPPY SPACE

Create a working environment that promotes focus, concentration and inspiration. Keeping your work area clean and orderly can help you to feel that you have things under control, while decorating it with pictures that evoke your work goals can help remind you why you come to work each day.

REWARD YOURSELF

When you complete a challenging project or successfully handle a tricky situation at work, self-congratulate with a treat. It could be splashing out on a restaurant meal or simply giving yourself a time-out from doing any household chores – just pick something that will motivate you to get through it. By preparing yourself for happiness in this way, you will already start to feel happy as you work toward it.

The fruit of
your own
hard work is
the sweetest.

Deepika Padukone

REFLECT ON THE
WORKING DAY

Each day as you finish work, set time
aside to sit quietly and think about what
has happened during the day. Write down
at least one positive thing to remind you
in future why your job matters to you.

EAT HAPPY

You are what you eat.

so eat for happiness.

GET YOUR HAPPY NUTRIENTS

Research has shown that eating food containing certain key nutrients can positively affect our mood. Get plenty of the following in your diet to keep your spirits up:

Calcium, found in dairy products, kale and other leafy greens like pak choi and spinach. A lack of calcium has been linked to low mood.

Magnesium, found in nuts, dark leafy vegetables, fish and wholegrain products. It can help to calm anxious jitters.

Chromium, found in broccoli, turkey, potatoes and wholegrain products. It helps the brain to regulate moods. The lack of it can lead to an increased risk of high blood pressure and depression.

B-vitamins are involved in the control of tryptophan (a building block for the mood-boosting chemical serotonin) and the production of GABA (gamma-aminobutyric acid), which also helps to elevate mood.

Zinc, found in seafood, eggs, beans, mushrooms, nuts, seeds and kiwi fruit. Studies have shown that low zinc levels are directly related to symptoms of depression.

Iron, found in dark-green leafy vegetables, meat, fish, beans, pulses, nuts and wholegrain products. It transports oxygen around the body and strengthens muscle. Depleted levels can lead to fatigue, low mood and depression.

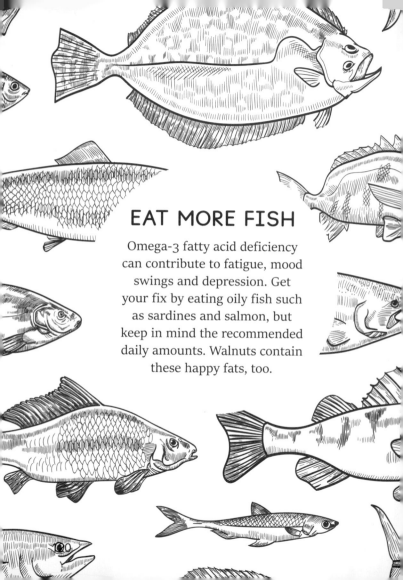

EAT MORE FISH

Omega-3 fatty acid deficiency can contribute to fatigue, mood swings and depression. Get your fix by eating oily fish such as sardines and salmon, but keep in mind the recommended daily amounts. Walnuts contain these happy fats, too.

ONE CANNOT
THINK WELL, LOVE
WELL, SLEEP WELL, IF ONE
HAS NOT DINED WELL.

Virginia Woolf

Happiness
comes

from within.

BALANCE YOUR MOOD WITH LOW-GI FOODS

Eating foods with a high GI (glycaemic index: the ranking of carbohydrate-containing foods based on their overall effect on blood glucose levels), such as sugary pastries and refined carbohydrates such as white bread, causes a spike in blood sugar. This then rapidly drops, leaving you tired and irritable. Eat low-GI foods instead, such as beans, rye bread and most fruit and veg. This will keep you off the blood-sugar rollercoaster and your energy levels and mood on an even keel.

STAY HYDRATED

Dehydration can leave you feeling
tired, irritable and even confused.
Keep water levels optimum by
drinking regularly throughout the
day. The recommended amount
is six to eight glasses, but that
can vary from person to person,
so listen to your body's needs.

COOK AT HOME

Research has shown that eating a healthy, home-cooked meal can make you feel better than splashing out on an indulgent meal at a restaurant. Home-cooked meals tend to be healthier, as you can choose exactly what you put in your food. And the process itself can be fun and mindful: just pick your favourite recipe, turn on the tunes and slip away in the moment. When you come back to reality there will be a tasty meal to demolish.

DECAFFEINATE

Caffeine inhibits the body's receptors of adenosine – a natural sedative that keeps us calm – which leads to feeling overstimulated. If you are prone to anxiety, the effects can be particularly bad for your mood. Reduce and replace caffeine intake gradually by switching to decaffeinated tea or coffee (which still contain some caffeine), then low-caffeine drinks such as green tea, and eventually caffeine-free options such as rooibos.

After a good dinner one
can forgive anybody,
even one's own relations.

Oscar Wilde

The best meals are those slowly savoured.

LOSE THE BOOZE

While sipping an alcoholic drink might initially help you to feel calm as endorphins (the body's feel-good drug) are released into your system, this can soon turn to anxiety once the alcohol wears off. Alcohol is also known to have depressant qualities, so by giving it a miss you will be avoiding the bad vibes and welcoming the good.

EATING WELL
IS THE HIGHEST
FORM OF
SELF-RESPECT.

ENJOY FOOD WITH FRIENDS OR FAMILY

Gathering around a table to eat together helps to establish and strengthen connections, which are vital to maintaining happiness and a sense of belonging. More to the point, it can be great fun! Instead of grabbing food on the go, make time at least once a week to catch up with friends or family over a healthy home-cooked meal.

134

IF MORE OF US
VALUED FOOD
AND CHEER AND
SONG ABOVE
HOARDED GOLD,
IT WOULD BE A
MERRIER WORLD.

J. R. R. Tolkien

MAKE PLATES THAT BRING SMILES

When it comes to food, presentation is
everything, so why not have some fun with it?
Make a vibrant salad popping with tomato reds,
pepper yellows and radish pinks, or arrange
your food on the plate in a smiley face.

EAT YOUR LUNCH OUTDOORS

Getting enough sunlight exposure is a daily bodily need, essential for the production of vitamin D, which is thought to aid the production of the mood-boosting chemical serotonin. If you spend most of the day indoors, either at work or at home, then you're probably not getting enough sunshine. When the weather allows it, taking a packed lunch to a park or eating at an al fresco café gives you a one-hour hit of light to get you through the day.

HAPPY BODY,
HAPPY MIND

GET ACTIVE

Studies have found that 20 minutes of exercise can positively affect your mood for up to 12 hours. It only takes a brief swim, brisk walk or a jog to trigger the release of mood-boosting endorphins and dopamine, and to reduce the production of stress hormones cortisol and adrenalin. That's why it makes you feel so good!

YOUR BODY IS THE GREATEST GIFT YOU WILL EVER RECEIVE. ENJOY AND CHERISH IT.

EXERCISE OUTDOORS

The fresh air, natural light and natural environment
will boost your mood more than exercising in
a sweaty gym. Try running, cycling or walking
in your local park, or something more gentle
and meditative such as yoga or t'ai chi.

FIND AN EXERCISE BUDDY

Teaming up with a friend is an excellent way to motivate yourself to get out and exercise. Besides the fact that it's more fun doing things together, it will hold you both accountable and so give you that extra incentive to take part. Or you could join a sports team or outdoor activity club and make some new friends along the way – many such clubs also organize social activities for members, so you'll be giving your social life a boost as well as getting fit. Win-win!

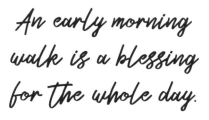

An early morning walk is a blessing for the whole day.

Henry David Thoreau

TRY YOGA

There is nothing like a good old stretching session to release muscle tension and help stress melt away. The ancient practice of yoga brings you more in touch with your body, thus helping you to feel more present in the moment. If you can, join a class in your area; otherwise, there are many YouTube yoga practitioners that you can follow for daily yoga routines that you can do at home.

HAPPINESS IS NOT A GOAL;
IT IS A BY-PRODUCT OF
A LIFE WELL LIVED.

Eleanor Roosevelt

Believe in yourself. You can do this!

IF YOU WALK
IN JOY,

HAPPINESS IS CLOSE BEHIND.

Todd Stocker

WALK A DOG

If you don't have your own pet, offer to walk one for
a friend or neighbour. Just getting out into the fresh
air will improve your mood, and dogs' enthusiasm
and joy for the simple pleasures in life is infectious.

PRIORITIZE SLEEP

If you're not getting enough sleep, you can suffer
from a weak immune system, slower reaction times
and be more prone to depression, anxiety and low
mood. Get into the habit of going to bed and getting
up at the same time, to ensure you get at least
eight hours' sleep a night. Adopt a nightly bedtime
routine to increase your chances of dropping off
with ease: stop using screen devices at least an hour
before bed and partake in a relaxing activity such
as reading or listening to music. Taking a hot bath
is also a good idea – the drop in body temperature
when you get out can help you to feel sleepy.

Sleep
is food
for the
soul.

MAKE YOUR BEDROOM
A SLEEP SANCTUARY

Decorate your bedroom in calming, neutral
tones, remove clutter and keep screens and
digital devices out. Invest in some cosy, inviting
bed linen and reserve the bedroom for sleeping
only. These things will help you associate the
room with a feeling of blissful relaxation.

EMPTY YOUR MIND OF WORRIES

Before you go to bed, make time to write down on paper anything that is worrying you and make a list of tasks for the next day. By doing this you will clear some headspace, allowing the mind to begin to relax. After doing the writing activity, you might also want to try spending some time in quiet meditation. This can be done very simply by sitting in a comfortable position, closing your eyes and focusing on your breath, letting the day's thoughts drain out of your mind.

A happy life consists in tranquillity of mind.

Marcus Tullius Cicero

IT'S THE
LITTLE THINGS

TAKE A BREATH
OF FRESH AIR

Step outside into nature and get a lungful of the
good stuff. The more fresh air you breathe in, the
more oxygen you take in, which in turn increases
the amount of serotonin in your system.

BEING HAPPY ISN'T HAVING EVERYTHING IN YOUR LIFE BE PERFECT. MAYBE IT'S ABOUT STRINGING TOGETHER ALL THE LITTLE THINGS.

Ann Brashares

LOOK UP AT THE STARS

Gazing up at the night sky can give an awe-inspiring sense of the vastness of the universe and our insignificance by comparison. This has a way of putting things in perspective – maybe your worries and problems aren't so big and bad as they seem. And studies have shown that experiencing this sense of awe can promote altruistic, helpful and positive social behaviour.

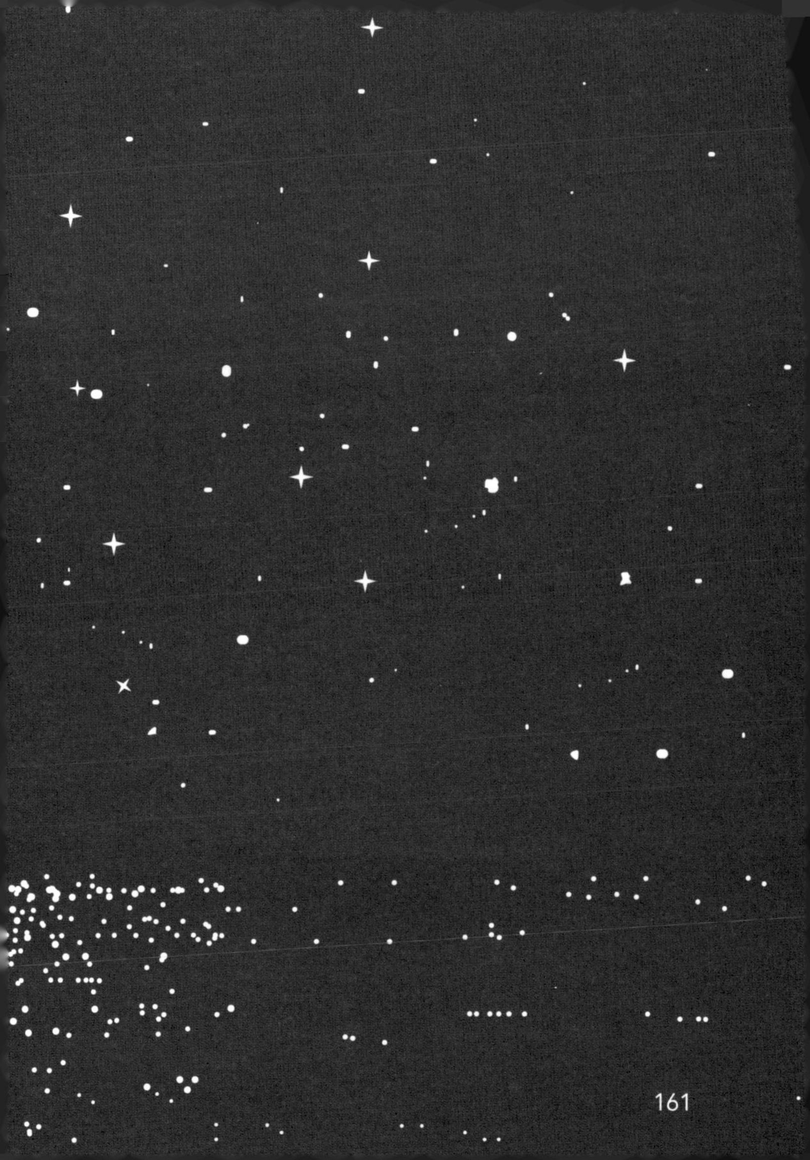

SMILE

Studies have shown that facial
expressions can enhance emotions –
so if you smile, your mood will begin
to match what your face is doing.
Smiling also releases endorphins,
the body's feel-good hormone.

TURN THAT FROWN

UPSIDE DOWN.

To live is the rarest thing in the world.
Most people just exist.

Oscar Wilde

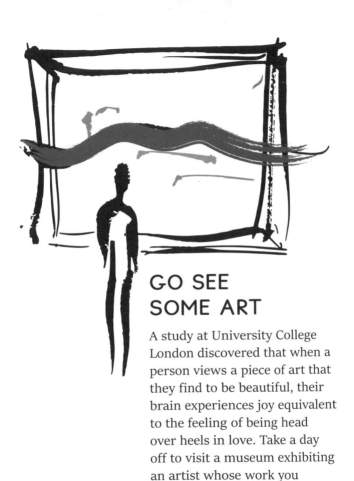

GO SEE
SOME ART

A study at University College
London discovered that when a
person views a piece of art that
they find to be beautiful, their
brain experiences joy equivalent
to the feeling of being head
over heels in love. Take a day
off to visit a museum exhibiting
an artist whose work you
find inspiring and beautiful.

CUDDLE A PUPPY OR KITTEN

Stroking a pet animal has been scientifically proven to lower blood pressure, reduce stress hormones and regulate heartbeat. It's pretty much impossible not to feel pure joy when playing with a furry companion.

DANCE

Dancing helps to spread positive energy through your body and to burn off not-so-positive pent-up energy and tension. Crank up your favourite tune full blast and just lose yourself in the moment.

JUST HAVE A GOOD TIME.

Happiness is a warm puppy.

Charles M. Schulz

LISTEN TO MUSIC YOU LOVE

Hearing your favourite music, particularly if
it's upbeat and uplifting, is an instant way to
bring a slice of happiness to your day. The act
of listening to music causes the brain to release
dopamine, a neurotransmitter that helps control
the brain's reward and pleasure centres.

IT IS NOT HOW MUCH WE HAVE, BUT HOW MUCH WE ENJOY, THAT MAKES HAPPINESS.

Charles Spurgeon

173

LET YOUR SOUL SING WITH JOY.

VISIT NEW PLACES

When you travel to a new country and see a
breathtaking view or are immersed in a culture you
have never before encountered, you experience "flow",
a state of mind whereby you are fully engrossed
in the moment, with energized focus and pure
enjoyment. Travel doesn't necessarily need to take
you far afield to fulfil this – even visiting a park
or city a few miles away will do the trick, as long
as it's somewhere you have never been before.

SPEND TIME NEAR WATER

They say that sea air is good for you, and that isn't just an old wives' tale. The negative ions released by the spray of thundering waterfalls and crashing waves are thought to help improve mood. Added to that, the sound of waves, the fresh air and the pleasing sense of smallness you get near a vast body of water are all likely to put you in a more chilled-out frame of mind.

HAPPINESS
THERAPIES

TRY MOOD-ENHANCING MEDITATION

The word "meditation" comes from the Latin *meditari* (to think, dwell on, exercise the mind) and *mederi*, to heal. At its simplest, it involves taking time out to sit still, away from distractions, and clear the mind of everyday thoughts. Meditation forms an integral part of many ancient spiritual practices, but it is as relevant to us today as it has ever been. The benefits are enormous: on the physical side, it lowers blood pressure and boosts the immune system, while on the emotional side, it helps us to combat stress. Setting aside time to meditate not only gives us a break from "doing", it allows us "to be" and to nurture our spirituality.

Anyone can learn to meditate. Start small:
find a quiet place to sit for a few minutes,
minimize any distractions and focus on your
breathing. With practice you'll find it easier
to meditate for longer periods of time.
If the idea of sitting in complete silence seems a
little off-putting at first, try a guided meditation:
an audio track that will talk you through a simple
visualization. (This is perfect if you're new to
meditating.) Some guided meditations will even
help you to explore a specific issue, such as stress
management or building self-confidence.

The present moment
is filled with joy
and happiness.
If you are attentive,
you will see it.

Thích Nhất Hạnh

REPEAT POSITIVE MANTRAS

Vocalizing thoughts gives them more substance; if you say it out loud, you are more likely to believe it yourself. Try repeating one of the following statements: "I am happy", "My life is full of good things", "I bring others joy". You could also write them down on postcards and display them around your home as a reminder.

My life is
full of
good things.

LOSE YOURSELF IN A GOOD BOOK

Studies have shown that reading for just six minutes can help to reduce stress levels significantly, and it works better and faster than listening to music or going for a walk. Some doctors prescribe books to treat depression, and there are even specialists, known as bibliotherapists, who provide tailored reading prescriptions listing specific books to help individuals to navigate the emotional challenges they face in life. It gives new meaning to the phrase "a good book"!

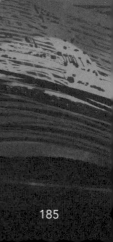

I DECLARE AFTER ALL THERE IS
NO ENJOYMENT LIKE READING!
HOW MUCH SOONER ONE TIRES OF
ANY THING THAN OF A BOOK!

Jane Austen

Tell yourself and the world you are happy.

LAUGH

A hearty laugh gets the blood flowing. And it just feels... good. Spend time with people who make you laugh, watch your favourite comedy show or relive a funny memory – whatever it takes to get those giggles going.

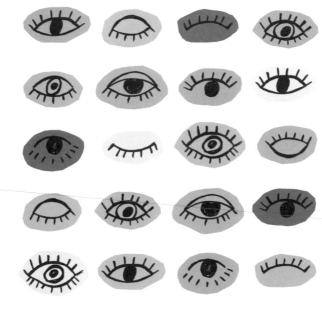

Now and then it's good
to pause in our pursuit of
happiness and just be happy.

Guillaume Apollinaire

TRY LAUGHTER YOGA

This unique brand of yoga involves prolonged bouts of voluntary laughter, which in turn become genuine, involuntary laughter. It's based on the theory that voluntary laughter can have the same health benefits as spontaneous laughter, namely, reducing stress hormone levels and lowering blood pressure, giving your immune system a boost, improving memory and having a positive effect on sleep patterns.

THE MOST IMPORTANT THING IS TO ENJOY YOUR LIFE

- TO BE HAPPY -

IT'S ALL THAT MATTERS.

Audrey Hepburn

IMAGE CREDITS

If you're interested in finding out more about our books, find us on Facebook at **Summersdale Publishers** and follow us on Twitter at **@Summersdale**.

www.summersdale.com